Jack In The Box

Gaelle Lacroix

Dedication

This book is dedicated to all those who have risen above self-doubt and defeatism, and are now working to encourage others to help themselves, too. I know how hard it is to put together broken hearts from my own experience, and I salute those who make it their mission to do this. Together, we can work to help others find self confidence and true happiness.

Acknowledgment

Life is full of blessings and I could take all day and count mine but my number one blessing is my son Eli. I would like to dedicate this book to and thank my son for being my inspiration and motivation to continue building myself and improving my knowledge to be able to provide a wonderful life for him. I can not thank him enough for putting smiles on my face daily and loving me unconditionally.

One day I hope my son reads this book and knows that he is the reason for everything good in my life. I would also like to thank my mother for allowing me to express myself and be myself despite the differences in opinions we may have had. The best gift she has given me is pushing me to always be the best that I can be and to let me know that I am my only limitation in life. Lastly, I'd like to thank God for giving me the strength to get through all my hurdles and struggles in life and letting me overcome them so that I am able to help others get through theirs.

About the Author

Mother, writer, dreamer, future lawyer, lover. As a young up and coming Haitian entrepreneur, Gaelle Lacroix knows it is important to help those around us because without this, we are nothing. In her spare time, Gaelle likes to give back to her community and feed and clothes the homeless.

Her dream is one day to be able to help young black children and mentor young minorities to understand the importance of getting an education and being able to rise above the stereotypes that society has bestowed upon them. Now-being a writer Gaelle hopes to influence others to love themselves unconditionally and find true happiness and peace within themselves through her writings.

Preface

Life is not meant to be easy. Everyone inevitably runs into obstacles. You can't let these hurdles bring you down. Disingenuous people are a renewable resource, and it is very easy to dig yourself into a hole. These are all struggles that are not unique to you; a lot of other people struggle with it as well.

The question then becomes, what will you do to change that? I once found myself in a similar situation, and I know exactly how easy it is to remain brooding in that cesspool and how difficult it can *seem* to pull out and fix what needs fixing. Because of that experience, I'm writing this book to let you know how you cannot just overcome your fears and anxiety, but how you can work towards your life's goals.

The advice that you will find in this book will be 100 percent honest and that means there might be some things that will hit a nerve within you. But that's the point, you need to realize what is wrong in order to fix it. So consider this you disclaimer, and read on.

Contents

Dedication i

Acknowledgment...ii

About the Author iii

Preface iv

Chapter 1 - Who are you? 1

Chapter 2 - Confronting and Transforming Your Fears ...10

Chapter 3 - Making Your Own Decisions..........................24

Chapter 4 - Breaking up with the Old You 34

Chapter 5 - Trusting Yourself...47

Chapter 6 - Taking The Risk And Going For What You Want..61

Chapter 7 - Loving Yourself Unconditionally 77

Quotes of Inspiration 94

Page Left Blank Intentionally

Chapter 1 - Who are you?

Have you ever thought, actually thought, about where you are headed? What you want to do? What is your purpose in life? These are the questions that plague the mind of almost everyone. There is nothing that one can do to escape these questions, especially if that 'one' is looking to make something of himself. Even if they are not looking to make something of themselves, this is still a question to which an answer is necessary.

The question remains, how does one realize their purpose in life? This is not something that develops overnight. Figuring out our purpose in life and finding out who we truly are and who we want to be is not something that is easy to do. It takes a lot of time, self-reflection and investing in ourselves for us to get to the bottom of this question.

There is a time limit to finding one's purpose in life, which is true. Although, the way we go about it is amazingly wrong. Societal pressure has been a key factor in how a person decides to spend their life. This results in the same deadened approach to life. It looks something like this; born, school, college, job, retirement, pension, and finally, the sweet embrace of death. This is the lifestyle that was followed for so long, but is now slowly changing. There is a time limit to this: at least, as far as risk-taking with minimal damage is concerned. These are your twenties. In this time of your life, you can work non-stop. Your sleep is non-existent and you can handle amazing amounts of pressure. This is the time to build your life, and the people who don't utilize this time efficiently are often those who end up mostly unsatisfied with their way of life or their occupation.

However, even if you did not take the time out in your twenties to do this, it is not too late to make the necessary changes to truly live out your purpose and find out who you really are. The best time to take risks and figure out who you are and what you want for yourself is NOW! I cannot begin to tell you how many of my friends are nurses for the simple reason that their parents put it in their minds from the minute they were born that the only way they will have job security and success is being a nurse! I can even remember my mom trying to beat that idea into my head when I was a child.

However, I myself knew that this just wasn't the path I wanted to take. Now don't get me wrong, nurses are amazing people and they do amazing things by saving lives. They are necessary in our society. However, that is not the only job that can provide fulfillment and success. To appease their family, they go down this path and do what they need to do to fulfill the requirement that their PARENTS expect of them, which is fine if that is what they truly want to do.

The problem lies in the fact that when they (not all) have to clock into work every day and they are unhappy and unsatisfied with what they are doing. Yes, they may be getting a paycheck, but their souls, their true desires, and their needs are not fulfilled. When people are offered something that may be risky but exciting and fills their soul with happiness, or something that is boring but safe and makes ends meet, they choose the safer option.

If you think to yourself that this person is stepping up to his or her responsibilities, you are mistaken. No they are not. The thing is, they made the decision based on what is right for others and not on what is right for them. I truly believe, however, that if you do the things that you truly want to do and are passionate about them, you will always gain success from them. If in your heart and soul, your passion is to be a nurse, you will be the best nurse ever. You will be happy and will make ends meet. However, if your passion is to be a fashion designer and you go for it full-force despite not having the *"security"* that a nurse may have, you will still be the best fashion designer ever. You will also be happy and will make ends meet. There may be an underlying cause to this. People are conditioned to think that the decisions that are made for them are only going to last for a moment, and the feeling of elation and jubilation will cease to exist.

The simple analogy that if a person does what he or she likes, they will never go to work a day in their lives, is true. That basically means doing what a person wants to do. What they want to do is affected by a lot of factors in their lives; their family upbringing, the people they make friends with, the types of teachers they get in their lives, or even their religion. All the choices that they made following every one of these aspects are the choices that they want you to follow, not what you want to do.

Although their and your interest might align, and you may actually find your passion this way, statistics suggest otherwise. Since most people have their choices influenced in some way or the other by people, and the greater number of people are unsatisfied with their job or their career, it is logical to assume that their interests are not aligning. Throughout their lives, people hold themselves back from making decisions purely because of what people may think. They do this in their job, if they have a job and they are being paid well, but they want to do something else. The only reason that they won't up and quit their job is because of what their parents, friends, and other people might think (We are not going to take into account those who may have families that they are a sole provider for, like children or spouses, because they might be sticking to their job to take care of their family, which is understandable).

I am talking about those that do not bear all the responsibility for their family. They are giving their time, energy and resources to a job they hate just because if they don't, they are going to get fired and eventually replaced. The fear of hearing people whisper behind your back, *"He had such a good job, but he just quit it,"* and *"You're a quitter,"* is powerful. It is enough to make anyone stay in a toxic environment. What they don't know is just how many times in a day you say to yourself, *"I hate my job."* The people you have in your life come to expect something of you when you are making a certain amount of money.

It may be a certain lifestyle that they get to enjoy on your expense, or just plain genuine concern for you. All these reasons make them resent you for quitting, even though you were miserable. Apart from professional life, in which the problems faced by men and women are mostly the same, in personal life, staying in toxic environment is something that women go through much more than men. There is an entire population of women who are staying in marriages for the simple reason that if they leave, people are going to say that she is a divorcee.

Or if a woman has a child, she will feel pressurized to marry the guy who fathered it, even if he doesn't treat her properly, just so that people won't gossip that she is not with the father of her child. Making these decisions based on other's opinions could be destructive to our lives and our happiness. Imagine everyone around you is happy EXCEPT YOU because you've done things based off of their opinions instead of what you really feel is best for you. All this may cause you to think that all other people are dumb and you should only do what you want.

That is not the case! **There is a fine line between taking advice from people and laying down and letting them walk all over you**. In fact, we do need guidance in order to go through life, but the people whom we trust and accept guidance from need to actually have experience from which we can benefit. The things that do make you happy and content should be your priority, and since nobody knows you better than yourself, you need to be the one with the final say.

Since you have been preconditioned to believe what others have told you about yourself, changing yourself is much harder than it is supposed to be. You cannot reasonably accept the fact that change is easy when you have spent your entire life a certain way and realize that practically, you have been spending it in a way that has only been beneficial to someone else's happiness.

When you realize the fact that you are not happy with

who you are, you will also learn that you aren't happy with the people in your life. This leads to a snowball effect. You are unhappy with your life, you're depressed and angry, and that leads you to being angry and unhappy with everyone in your life, including yourself. This causes you to become the very person you hate, as you will begin channeling your frustration into controlling other people's lives, too. The unhappiness is something that stems much deeper than what is on the surface. There're many things that you have to consider and focus on so that you are able to truly make the decisions and be who you are really meant to be in this life. Remember, the most important person in your life is YOURSELF.

If you listen to any successful person and the advice that they give, it is what you already know. The things that they applied in their lives are the things that have already been taught to us and are mostly common sense. These things or traits that successful people adopt are mostly very basic and go without saying. So why can't a normal person apply these things into their lives. The simple answer to this is that it is just too hard. The amount of self-control that a person must possess is amazing in order to even stick to a schedule for one month, let alone their entire lives.

To become disciplined and assertive, people need to go through an entire process that is almost as hard as achieving your goal. What we need to remember is that when we go through the process of change, we expect there to be success at the end of the tunnel. This is not always the case. At the end of the tunnel, you will find a ladder to success. You have to now start climbing this and put your foot on the ladder's first step.

Chapter 2 - Confronting and Transforming Your Fears

We all have fears in our lives. Some may be due to a childhood trauma, some may be irrational, and some may be due to a particular event that happened at some point in your life. There is no one alive who is fearless and doesn't have anything they are afraid of. Though, there are people who can be perceived as fearless as they are very good at hiding or confronting their fears.

When people hear the word, the things that pops into their mind is arbitrary stuff like: spiders, heights, darkness and that sort of thing. Though these are valid fears and should be taken into account, there are also emotional fears that need to be thought about. These are fears like losing people closest to you, not living up to your potential, even though you are doing everything you can to make sure that that does not happen, leading a life that is useless, getting left behind, and many more.

The baseline of these fears, however, remains the same. Every fear needs to be dealt with similarly. The only way to conquer a fear is to face it outright and to face it without any hesitation. Imagine yourself in a battlefield. You against a thousand of your opponents. You know that you cannot run back, nor can you surrender. The only thing left is to fight. You know that there is no alternative and no way out. Either way, one side has to win: you or your opponents.

Life and fear follow a similar analogy. It's you against all your fears. These may be anything, and they will leave you powerless and will leave you without any will power to live life. What is the use of a life that is ruled by fears? You need to sit down and assess how many opportunities you have let go or how many shots you have missed just because you were too afraid of the outcome.

The experiences you miss will eventually pile up and one day, when you think back to it, you will realize what a great life you missed out on. There is nothing more daunting than the thought of looking back and thinking that you should have tried more or experienced more. One of the most common need of humankind is to have companionship. There is a growing fear of humiliation.

Do you remember that girl or boy that you saw at a party, but were too afraid to go up to her and ask her or him out? It may have been because you thought that they were out of your league, because you were not in a good place in life or that you thought that they would never even consider a person like yourself. Without any hint whatsoever, you made up a judgment in your mind that you are not good enough, because of whatever reason. You did not even attempt to give yourself a shot. If we put it in another way, you deprived yourself of the opportunity at a new experience.

You didn't know what that new experience would bring. It may have been happiness, or it may have been sadness. If you think about it, isn't that the case with every decision that you make? Then why shy away from this? If we talk about the stereotypes between the genders, there are different reasons this happens. Men are more prone to be self-conscious of approaching women, because they don't want to get the rejection from her side.

The above-mentioned reasons apply to both men and women, but in most cases, men are the ones who suffer from low self-esteem. There is social pressure that men have to be the providers for women. Let me tell you something: in this day and age, women are more than happy to be equal contributors in the finances of the family. Even though it does differ from person to person, due to recent progress thanks to feminism, there is growth seen in women empowerment and them wanting to be the ones who are equal partners. When it comes to women, the reasons are mainly centered on looks or a certain type of men they have dealt with in the past. They tend to paint every men with the same brush, and consider that if a person is in a particular field or they have a certain interest, then they are bound to turn out to bad. That is also not the case.

The whole process of finding someone to spend one's life with is a trial and error method. You might be able to find someone that is everything that you don't like, but the way that they manage it and treat you forces you to reconsider your priorities. Even if you're conscious of your looks, then what? Don't you deserve to be happy? Don't you deserve what is best for you? Maybe your partner doesn't think as much about looks as they think about personality.

Everything in this case is basically trial and error, with the baseline being that it is not the right way to refrain yourself from being happy just because of an assumption about other person's mentality or because you think that you are not good enough. There will always be a reason for not going for it, but there will also be a reason to go for it. It sounds a bit confusing, but the point remains the same. You just need to change your perspective. Where most people tend to focus on the negatives, focus on the positive instead. If you focus on your fears and assess them as aspects of your life, you will realize that there is a fair chance that it is because of someone else. The way you feel about your looks, the feeling of incompetency you get in your professional life, the complex you suffer from whenever you compare yourself to other people, and more, are all the products of someone else's mind, not yours'.

Think about it, who is the problem here? The way you feel about your looks, you feel that way because someone made you feel that way. The feeling of incompetency you get in your professional life is because your superiors made you feel that way. They may have a valid point that your work is not up to the mark, but that is not the problem. The problem arises when you are made to feel less competent than others, instead of being helped. Now consider all these problems and think about what they are stopping you from achieving. The way you look could be holding you back in your personal life.

You need to learn that not everything is about your looks, though this does not mean that you need to stop focusing on maintaining yourself. Just realize that not everything is centered on looks. Just the feeling of not being attractive is holding you back from being happy and shying away from everyone and isolating yourself is never the answer. Forget what people think about you and realize the insignificance of the comments is the way to go.

Another way of thinking about this is that it is an opinion. Everyone has them, and you don't have any responsibility to change them. So why bother yourself about them at all? The fear of rejection or humiliation has held you back from achieving happiness and for what reason? Because of being laughed at?

"If a problem is fixable, if a solution is such that you can do something about it, then there is no need to worry. If it is not fixable, then there is no help in worrying. There is no benefit in worrying whatsoever"

-Dalai Lama

If you feel incompetent in your professional life, there could be a couple of reasons for that. Firstly, you need to know that if you are lacking in your professional life, then it is probably because there are underlying factors. Problems are not created in a vacuum. The underlying factors can pertain to your personal life, feuds you have with your superiors, and those sorts of common things. It could also be because your work is not up to the mark that is required. In that case, there is no other way except to improve.

If it is because of your personal life, then there you need to work on confronting your fears. You have let your fears rule your life so much that they have encroached upon your professional life. The factor that is lacking is the happiness that you achieve from the satisfaction of having a stable personal life. If there is no satisfaction, then there is no motivation to work. Thus, you feel incompetent and everything seems that much more depressing.

If you have an unhappy mind, then there is no way that you can expect there to be any productivity in your work. If you feel a complex when you are comparing yourself to other people, it may be because they are making more money than you are. They are in a better position in life than you are. Ask yourself, how did they get there? Are they really in a better position than you are? Is it at all possible that they have their own battles to fight and that they are fighting them? The only thing that you need to realize is that all the trials and tribulations you face in your life are meant to be fought. They are not there just so you can see them and do nothing about it. Everything in life has a cost. The cost of happiness is simply working as hard as you can to achieve it.

It includes going out of your comfort zone, aiming high, and then working towards it. How do you achieve all of that? The answer is as simple as this; you need self-confidence. That is probably the most clichéd line there is. Get self-confidence and then everything will fall into line, and your life will automatically sort itself out. That is not the case, as getting self-confidence is the first step into being in a stable state of mind that you need to be in order to achieve happiness.

"Don't wish for an easy life, wish for the strength to live a

hard one"

-Bruce lee

Bruce Lee aptly said that an easy life is not worth living. If you have an easy life, then there is no way to let go of that feeling of incompetency that you feel. There is always the added aspect of being a bit better, but that better is always on the other side of your comfort zone. In order to achieve that life, you need to have the assurance that you are worthy of it. That assurance comes from knowing and understanding your self-worth. If you yourself don't think you are worth anything, then how would you expect anyone else to think that you are worth anything?

Nobody that you know is a mind reader. Nobody knows how you feel, the anxiety you feel, or the problems you face. They only know about you: what you know, what you say, and how you look. You can look like the most confident man or woman in the world, and people will believe you, simply because you look the part. Faking confidence is the best way to actually being confident. There are no if, or, or but's in this part. To achieve even a modicum of happiness, you need confidence.

The confidence we are talking about is not the one that makes you boastful or makes you a jerk. It is just the self-assurance that a person has in order to deal with anyone and everyone so that nobody can get you down or make you feel inferior. There are two categories of people who do this; those who love to hide behind the mask of anonymity or those who you have let into your life so that they have an open ground to make you feel inferior to them.

As for the people who have no importance in your life, ask yourself, why does their opinion matter at all? Why should they have a say? Even the things they are saying, how do they know what they are talking about since they don't know you, nor do they have any idea what you have been through. It has been noted by psychologists that being superior gives people a feeling of elation. The easiest way to feel superior is by putting other people down.

So if you think about it, they are actually making

themselves feel better at your expense. There is no reason to take anything these people say seriously. They have no clue as to how they can get their own lives in order, so for a feeling of momentary happiness they put others down. The superiority they get is short lived and has no effect on their lives, whatsoever. However, it has also been noticed that by helping other people, the feeling of elation is bit more permanent and the only reason that more people don't do this is because it is harder. It is so hard to help other people than to put them down. The people whom you have let into your life and they put you down, there may be a reason for that. Maybe they aren't in a good place and are following the train of thought of putting others down to make themselves feel superior. There are two ways to go about this. You can either help them out, or you can cut them out of your life.

If you are going to help them out, then a good method to approach this would be disassociation. In this method, you basically disassociate them from yourself and whatever they say just bounces off of you and makes no impact. Their words become meaningless. Approaching the problem this way has a twofold result. You can bear whatever they say about you, and then help them sort their own lives out. If you think that they have crossed a line, you can just cut them out.

Keep in mind that you owe nothing to anyone and whatever friendship you might have had with that particular individual was finished when they started giving you second-hand resentment from their own lives. Don't ever be afraid to confront your fears, whether it's a bad friendship that you need to cut out and are too afraid of their reaction, or if it is going for a job that you really want but you're afraid of the risks that may come with it. Fear comes in between true happiness. After all, the goal is to find your true happiness in this life and being afraid to do the things that you want to do will always stand in the way of that happiness. All the fears that you may have in different aspects of your life need to be transformed into the confidence that you need to make decisions for yourself and by yourself.

If you always have to ask for a million different opinions, when it is time for you to do something that you like or want, then that means you fear the outcome and in turn, you are allowing other people to make your decisions for you based on what they want for themselves and not what YOU want for yourself. Have you ever thought that maybe, the fears that you have about a certain things are someone else's fears that they have put in your mind to stop you from doing what truly makes you happy, just because they are afraid? Let us take children as an example.

They are truly fearless creatures. They see something that they like or something that they want to do, and they go for it uninhibited. It is not until their parents or other adults tell them no or make them feel like what they're doing is wrong or dangerous that they start developing fears or being hesitant about doing something that they wanted to do instinctively. This is a prime example of what happens when you want to do something, and someone shuts your dreams down by putting fears into your head by telling you things like, *"If you start this business, you won't make any money," "There're so many makeup artists now that there's no place in the market for you,"* or *"You should dress like this as that's the new trend going around."*

I remember having conversations with one of my friends,

and she would tell me all of these great ideas of what she wanted to do with herself. The problem was that every time she would mention her ideas about what she wanted to do, she would follow that with a 'BUT'. Then, she would proceed to name all of the negatives and cons about what may happen if she chooses that path. If you catch yourself doing the same thing, then you need to realize that small itty-bitty word 'but' is the fear that is holding you back from achieving your true happiness and accomplishing the things that you want for yourself. Fear also tends to hide itself in the form of comparing yourself to others. When thinking of doing something and you look at someone else, remarking, *"So and so tried to do this but it didn't work for them,"* you're automatically instilling that fear of someone else's failure in yourself. Remember that that person isn't you and you are not that person. Everyone's journey and outcome is different!

Chapter 3 - Making Your Own Decisions

The first thing we have all been taught before we make a decision is to gather information so that we are able to make an informed choice. The information that we gather, or the advice that we seek, is a risky thing. It is a double-edged sword, which many of us use to harm ourselves as we are usually not able to discern between the advice we should take and the advice that is better left alone. The bottom line here is to understand that what we are calling advice is merely a suggestion.

The suggestion then can be classified as advice once it is determined that the suggestion has not come from a place of self-interest. People, when receiving advice, do not pause to break it down to understand the nature of the advice being given. You have to be able to discern what is genuinely meant to help you or what is merely a suggestion coming from a place of personal preference. When you are open to suggestions, you usually do not get to do what you would like to.

Rather, you have to fall in line with what the other person wants and is comfortable with. The question is how to find the right balance between being open to suggestions and knowing when to just pull away and start doing the thing that makes you happy. How many times has it happened that you did not take your normal route to work or home, because your friend in the passenger seat had some advice or suggestion to share on the route they found more comfortable?

How many people do you know have joined certain professions, just because their parents advised them to? How many individuals are avoiding something, just because they have been advised that it is not in their best interest? There is a difference between advice that is given out of self-interest, and advice that is given from a genuine place of wanting something better for the other person.

What we as advice-seekers need to understand is that it is solely up to us to take what we want, and discard the rest of it. Although it is true that it is easier said than done, most of the times what happens when we are upset or angry is that our perceptions get blown way out of proportions. Something that we might have been able to easily shrug off might bother us a lot when we are confronted with it during a time of stress. Even though there is a grain of truth in our anger and irritation, our reaction just does not justify it. Mostly, we can all acknowledge that our reactions were blown up once we have calmed down. However, this grain of truth remains, and it is really frustrating when someone comes along and tries to deny that the truth even exists. Most of the time, you might be able to shrug off these comments. But sometimes, they really take root in your thoughts, and the result is devastating.

You begin to question your own judgment, you question your decisions, and you do not know anymore whether or not you are doing anything right at all. This is especially true if this denial comes from a figure of authority. For example, it is easier for us to shake off the comments and views of family members if they differ from our own, but it is a lot harder to ignore them when those opinions come from people who have studied professionally about it; like doctors and professors.

It is extremely important for us to consider advice that might seem bad for us, but is necessary for our improvement. On the other hand, it is equally important that we learn to recognize that the people giving us advice might be mistaken, or more truthfully, they might not even be aware of what is happening around us. Therefore, anything they have to add becomes totally worthless.

Another aspect of advice that you need to be conscious about is that most people will give you advice that is just coming out based on their own experience. For example, my friend told me a story about a time where she was going on a trip. When the plane took-off for her flight, she started to feel sick and nauseous: like she wanted to throw up. Mind you, she has been on plenty of flights and this is the first time she's ever felt like this. The guy seated next to her asked her what was wrong.

Even though he seemed genuinely concerned, when she told him that she was feeling nauseous, he automatically jumped into a longwinded story about how he overcame his anxiety about flying and convinced her that she was just having anxiety and that it was nothing to worry about. Long story short, she had a stomach virus and that was the reason for her feeling like this. Had she listened to him and ignored that feeling and not make her own judgment and decision about what was wrong, who knows what may have happened. Even though this is an obvious example of how people usually do not try to even scratch the surface of what is wrong in their life, know that everyone stands at the ready to offer you advice. People usually try to silence your thoughts and questions with false ideas of comfort. When someone is asking you to do a certain thing, they more often than not have a vested interest in your decisions.

The best thing to do is ask yourself why they want you to do a certain thing, even though your gut is telling you not to. You will be surprised by how many times the answer you arrive at will indicate the fact that the people who are giving you a particular advice are only making you do something because it would benefit them somehow.

This is the most basic reason why when you have a decision to make, it is best to listen to everyone's advice and then go with your gut feeling. It is a fatal mistake to listen to advice and be so swayed by it that it rules over all your actions from then onwards. You might want to take advice that seems great, especially if it is coming from a loved and trusted source. But does that mean that you should just take that advice and then simply go along with the flow? No, absolutely not! You are ultimately not the one then who is making a decision. Rather, a decision was made for you and you are simply following it through. What happens when down the road, you figure out that the advice you so willingly followed, and somehow convinced yourself was something you wanted as well, is something you never had any interest in doing all along?

Just like it is important to realize that the decision that you are taking is going to impact your life, it is also important to realize that if you have been corralled into taking a decision that is not in your best interest, you always have the option of turning back. Take that as a lesson learned and retrace your steps back.

You Always Have the Option of Starting Over

Furthermore, it is your duty to yourself to challenge everything you hear under the umbrella of advice. You have to be adamant in questioning everyone's motive. You should also continuously remind yourself of what you want. If at some point, you are not sure of what it is that you want, you have to devise ways that will open you up to thinking in ways that makes clear to you what it is that you want to do. For this, it is especially important to trust your instincts. You should always remember that this is YOUR life and it is going to be your choices and decisions that are going to dictate where you end up. The question most probably in your mind right now must be, *"What if I am afraid of making a decision?"*

Well, the answer is simple; fear can be a good thing! You can use your fear to remind yourself that you are afraid because you are breaking the norm. Standing up for what you believe in is going to be a little bit terrifying, but it will ultimately shape who you are. In other words, it is totally worth it in the end.

If you have analyzed and questioned your decision, and trust it to be what you think it is, that you know the decision you are taking is something that you want and you yourself have researched its pros and cons, and are informed enough, then you should just take that leap of faith.

Show Yourself that You Believe in You

You should never undermine your own confidence by letting go of the reins, even a little bit. That little bit can only just be you getting influenced by someone, whose opinions you value, into doing something you are not sure about. There really is nowhere you can look where you would find the perfect answer on how you should make decisions. Everyone can guide you, but the effort has to come from within. You have to be willing to confront a few realities and go through some difficult introspection. If you are honest with yourself, then you have in your mind and heart found answers that you were looking for outside.

The best course of action, when confronted with a major decision, is to look inwards. That is the best place from where to get all your answers. The reason for that is, YOU ARE THE ONE WHO HAS TO LIVE WITH YOUR DECISIONS. If you fall into the trap of following the advice of someone else, which did not jibe with your interest, then even though you can go back and start over, you will have wasted precious time.

This wastage could have been avoided if only you had taken time out to analyze your thoughts and desires. People will always tell you to learn from others' mistakes, and this is true to some extent. But you also have to remember that not everyone is going to face a similar situation in their life as you. Let us suppose that the situations were similar; even then, you cannot possibly learn from that person's' situation. That is because you both are different. When the situation is similar, your reactions might be totally different. When that person might have reacted by giving up and suffering a loss, you might be the one to persevere and gain rewards. Another reason you should always try to make your own decision is that you do not want to spend your life blaming another person for the predicament that you are in.

No matter what you have decided to do, you are likely to put in more effort into trying to succeed if you are the one who made the decision. If you made the decision based on someone else's opinion, you are very likely to just give up and resort to blaming that person for wasting your time. As social creatures, we should all understand that we would function a lot better if we understood that there are boundaries that need to be respected, even within familial units.

Making decisions, letting others make decisions, and trying to be supportive without being opinionated or judgmental, is something we should all strive towards achieving. Everyone should be allowed to make their own decisions. We should not interfere, nor invite others to interfere, with this.

"It is far better for a man to go wrong in freedom than to go right in chains."

-Thomas H. Huxley-

Chapter 4 - Breaking up with the Old You

It is never easy trying to please those around you. I unfortunately got into the habit of pleasing people as a way to avoid drama. Let me tell you that for all those people out there, this is how it starts. The vice is adopted with just the innocent intention of either trying to avoid drama or trying to please those around you because you love them. Although your intention is to avoid confrontation and drama, what happens with this approach is that you end up being the doormat.

When you do not voice your opinion, you become the push over. You become the person who is easy and gullible. This is how it all began; I started trying to please those around me. I simply wanted to live in harmony with those around me. I wanted to establish an energy around me that attracted people and made them want to stay. However, what ended up happening is the exact opposite of that. Instead of finding that, people appreciated my tendency to put their needs before mine.

Soon, I became surrounded by people who were extremely controlling, rude and selfish. Their opinion, which was very obvious from their behavior towards me, was that I was not to be respected because I was the sort of person who did not have an opinion of her own. It is true that in my pursuit to become a drama-free individual, I had become someone who did not know where her voice ended and the voice of those around her started.

Instead of becoming relaxed and happy that my life was free of drama, the current reality was now even more confusing. This can be a very vicious cycle; this thought that you get of trying to please those around you. Like I said, it starts off simply and very innocently. But sooner than you are able to process what is happening, you are ensnared by the vicious thoughts of those around you. It doesn't matter that you are making all this effort for them; they just start thinking of you as gullible or a push over.

Instead of being the person who you are deep down, the true you remains buried. You adopt the beliefs and thought processes instilled within you by society. The people who you cared a lot for are now thinking that you do not have any opinion worth sharing. They will not look at the humane effort you are making in order to make their lives comfortable. Once you are in this position, instead of getting out of it, you start feeling rejected. The reason you started doing this probably started with someone you cared. But instead, what you got in return was ridicule, and you lost your self-respect to boot. Instead of going back to the way you were before, you start asking why the people around you behave in such a demeaning manner. You want the answer to this mind-boggling question.

For me, it was like this. Once I started on the path to becoming a people pleaser so that they would find comfort around me and know that I value their opinion, their reactions towards my behavior was astounding. I was left with this raging fire of despair. Why do the people I care about so much not see that I am trying to value their opinion? How could someone be so clueless?

What I did after that was even more self-harming. I continued in my ways, thinking that those who were currently around me were the ones who did not understand me. I made excuses that maybe they were not mature enough to understand the effort I was making for them. Turns out, I was the one deluding myself through all of it. It was I who had the wrong approach towards making my life drama-free, as well as showing my love and care through my actions. The actions I adopted were the wrong ones, too. It took me a lot of heartbreak and depression to figure out that it was those imposed ideals and concepts, which were forcefully instilled upon me by the people around me and society, which were at fault here. I had to learn how to become my true self and kick that people pleaser personality out of me.

Your Thinking and Way of Life is Never Wrong, You just Need to Apply it a Bit Better

On this journey to becoming my true self, I realized that I needed to change the application of my thinking. I was confronted with yet another problem. I had become comfortable within the space I had made for myself. I discovered that this people pleasing personality residing within me had overstayed its welcome and now, I am used to this entire ordeal.

Even though I was stuck, I was more terrified of change than I was of everything else that came with my situation. This, more than anything else, astonished me. How is it possible for someone in my situation to not want to come out of it? I discovered that people usually become defensive when it is suggested to them that they should change themselves. Even though change is the one thing that remains constant in the universe, most people refuse to accept it as the reality of life. They refuse to acknowledge that change is the one thing that makes sense if you want to MOVE FORWARD IN YOUR LIFE.

The astonishing fact is that people choose to remain in their miserable states, just out of fear of change. They get comfortable with being mediocre, just because they are afraid of what change might bring. I was being one of these people.

Everything Changes Whether Anyone Wants to Accept it or Not

I also figured out that people that are in search for better lives should first accept that the only way it is going to happen is through change. There is no way around it. If you want a better life, you are going to have to accept that you will need to change the things around yourself, and not just once. It has to be a process, wherein you are continually changing your environment and trying your best to take it in the direction your inner-self envisions. It is of the utmost importance that those who want to actively improve their lives accept that the only way it will happen is through change. Since I was looking to change one self-destructive habit after another, I decided to take it one small step at a time. What I knew for sure was that I wanted to change the situation that I was in. Since I was committed to making my situation better, accepting change was easier. Below, I will list a few things that I found helpful during this time of transition.

Accept Uncertainty

You have to accept that being uncertain is a part of life. The sooner you understand how to cope with it, the better you will be prepared to deal with change, initiated or otherwise. You should also make it a habit to let go of things that you have no control over. The things you cannot influence must not make you fear change either. They will be there regardless of whether you decide to change or not.

Look At Possibilities

What would you get if you went with the change and instead lost everything? What would the situation be like? What if the worst thing that can happen when you initiate a change is not the result of the change that you initiated, rather a change that was forced upon you? How would you react to it then? This question will help you plan for possible backup plans, taking out some of the anxiety associated with change.

Start Small

Whenever you are looking to change something about yourself, you should always start small. Change is already hard; you should not make it harder on yourself by trying to change everything at once.

Be Patient

The next thing you should do is be patient with change, as well as yourself. You need to give time for everything to fall into place. You cannot expect yourself to change a habit that took years developing to just change overnight.

Do Not Think About Failure

If you are starting something while anticipating failure, then it is bound to happen. Furthermore, when you are focusing all your energy on wondering how you can fail, you are not thinking enough about how it could all succeed.

If you want to imagine possibilities, imagine the positive ones.

Do Not Look Back

Looking back is what prevents you from moving ahead. If you keep looking back, you will have a hard time adjusting with the new environment ushered in by change. When you have already made the decision to move ahead and initiate change, then looking back is of no use. You should move ahead with confidence and never look back. Be sure that what is over is over.

Once the Human Brain is accustomed to a Situation, It is Very Hard to Let Go of It

I discovered the truth of this statement while I was in the process of taking baby steps towards my own change. However, I want to say that if you analyze the true nature of change, you will understand that when you are actually thinking about changing some aspect of yourself or your life, your mind and emotions go through a few phases. The first thing that you experience is some variation of excitement. It is the same anticipatory feeling you get after buying something new. You are either anticipating that it will improve the quality of your life, and that has you excited, or it could be that you have brought new clothes and are looking forward to wearing them. Anyways, the point is that no matter what you buy, your mind is anticipating how you are going to use it and incorporate it into your life. The same thing happens when you plan on changing some aspect of your life. You are freed from the shackles of the past. You transform into your true self. You are filled to the brim with positivity and you are looking forward to it. No matter how much anticipation you have in your thoughts, more often than not, this excitement makes us overlook some gritty details about the change that we are trying to implement.

Hence, I focused all my energy on the anticipation of change. I no longer wanted to be the person who was thought of as a doormat. I wanted people around me to respect me and my opinions. I no longer wanted to be the person who got overlooked just because she cared about the comfort of others. I understood through all those years of being a people pleaser that no one was coming to return the favor.

I was waiting for someone out there to realize that I was not someone who was a pushover. I wanted them to realize that I did have opinions. I just wanted them to be able to voice theirs. Well, since I realized that this approach of mine was not working, I figured that I would try to become the person who takes care of herself first. If no one was going to return the favor, then I was going to extend it only intermittently. I realized through a lot of disappointments and heart breaks that the only person who was going to help me was me. The only genuine way out of my predicament was to start becoming aware of my internal world. It was to become more aware of myself, as well as my needs and opinions. I was the only one who could give me a voice and a space to be heard. Since it was me, after all, who took away my voice from myself.

Be Aware of Who You Are

I realized that the only way for me to come out of this soul crushing place, was to go into myself and take a look at who I was. I thought it would be beneficial for me to first find out who I was, and what it was that I wanted. Was I even really the person I thought I was? I wanted to answer all these questions and become more aware of myself as a person. I no longer wanted to live in denial of myself, nor did I want to live in the judgment of others. When I started doing this, it gave me a better idea of what drove me to please people. So when I was in a group of people, I was better able to handle the pulse and take a different direction.

Giving Too Much to a Relationship Hurts It

This may sound counter-productive, but it is true. I learned through experience that it is not true that you should give your all to a relationship. Even though you should be true, honest, loving and caring in your relationship, what you should not do is over-perform. When you do more than your share continually, you are encouraging the other person to underperform by default. This hurts the overall effectiveness of your relationships.

You Are Unique

When you understand that everyone is not made the same way and that you are different than others, and that holds no negative implications in your mind, then you have achieved a place of comfort in your mind.

Avoiding a Problem Does Not Make It Go Away

You have to realize that a problem simply does not go

away if you avoid thinking about it or do not try to resolve it. I tried avoiding difficult situations and conflicts too, instead of dealing with them. That is how I developed the habit of trying to please people. I wanted to avoid any drama, rather than deal with them.

Never Make Decisions When Anxious.

When you try to make decisions based on your anxiety, you are paving the way for more anxiety to enter your life. Any decision made during this time will not be what you want. It will just be a reaction and not a thought-out response. When I stopped making decisions while I was anxious, I saw my relations improving instantaneously.

Accept Who You Are

This is not to say that you should not try to make yourself better always. However, even in order to improve yourself, you first need to learn and accept who you are. You should understand that self-acceptance is a process, and it will continue throughout your life. Although, once you start, you will realize that the changes you experience are almost immediately visible in all aspects of your life.

Change does not come without effort. You have to realize

that what is happening is not having a positive impact and anything that does not affect your life positively needs to go. When the problem in your life is people pleasing, you need to realize that it is never too late to learn to live on your own terms. You need to realize that you are better off living a life on your own terms rather than the terms of those around you.

This is especially the case when your efforts do not mean all that much to them. When I realized that I needed to breakout of the people pleasing trap, I had to give up on my idea that people would change because of me. Yes, looking back now it seems rather naive of me to think that people would just change, all for me, when I would not change for myself. Society has imposed certain beliefs, which simply became a larger part of my life.

When I noticed the frightening drawbacks, I decided that enough was enough. I wanted to be able to enjoy my life being my true self. Anyone who wanted to join me then was more than welcome. These people pleasing habits were not going to stop me anymore. I decided to change *my* behavior, rather than expecting people to change theirs. I had to look after my happiness first. It holds a higher priority. Once I bid my old self *adieu*, and started living like my true self, life improved drastically for the better.

"Be Bold, be brave enough to be your true self"

-Queen Latifah

Chapter 5 - Trusting Yourself

"I got my own back."

-Maya Angelou

The type of environment that has been cultivated today makes it very difficult for people to be themselves. I want to make myself the guinea pig, and analyze my behavior and situation, when it was too difficult for me to actually be myself. It was just too hard to let go of the barriers that just naturally built up inside me as I grew up. Whether it was the atmosphere of high school or the behavior of the people around me, I was not quite sure during that phase.

For some inexplicable reason, I was afraid to goof around as much as I would have liked to, nor did I laugh to my heart's content. What I remember was that I was constantly stiff and uneasy about myself. I thought that I was not good enough. That most of my traits were better kept hidden. Then, this thinking of mine progressed to keeping most of my thoughts to myself as well.

What I was actually afraid of was getting rejected or shunned and shamed for being myself. I was afraid I would not be accepted by my peers. So instead of trying to find a better solution, I started to shun myself to avoid being shunned by others. I started not feeling comfortable in my own presence. I put on a show for myself, as well as for others, because to me, it felt like I was watching an actor perform. Most of the things I did was me putting up an act. I did consider myself an excellent actor, though.

I was able to monitor my emotions and reactions pretty well. However, what this act did was convince me that I was not good enough; that my beliefs, my thoughts, whatever made up the individual that I was, wasn't good enough. I did not acknowledge that I might have some genuine thoughts that were interesting and that needed to be voiced. It was always the fear of being ridiculed that kept my mouth firmly shut most of the time.

Indeed, I kept most of my emotions all locked up inside as well. Never for a moment in that time did it cross my mind that I might have the capacity to feel love more deeply than I allowed myself too, or that I might be more kind and wise than I knew. I never thought that living any other way was possible. To my understanding, letting go of my carefully constructed performance was inviting disaster. So I continued to live a condensed life, one that was closely monitored by myself. Everything as checked and verified by a template of behavior that I had carefully constructed before it was allowed outside. The result was that I fluctuated between being mostly numb to being in pain, although at the time I was not aware of it.

For me, that was the way life was. I thought that it was the price you had to pay to live a life that was free of fear. I was completely oblivious to the fact that the reason everything felt this surreal to me was because I was not letting myself live my life to its fullest potential. I was limiting myself because of fear, all the while thinking that fear was what lay at the other side of my freakish control.

"As soon as you trust yourself, you will know how to live."

-Johann Wolfgang von Goethe, Faust: First Part

As I grew older, I gradually began to realize that the real reason behind my distrustful exterior was that I did not trust myself. When I kept telling myself that the world, and by extension the people in it, were untrustworthy, the truth of the matter was that I did not trust myself to deal with it. I did not trust myself to take chances and deal with the consequences, nor did I trust myself to make mistakes and learn from them. What I had to unlearn over the course of many years was to not take myself so seriously all the time.

I had to learn from scratch the basics: even the fact that not everyone is perfect. We are flawed. It is the acceptance of those flaws and our efforts to correct them and learning to work with them that makes us uniquely us. There are some aspects of living the way I did that makes it sound appealing. However, those are only there for a limited amount of time. In the long-term, they only serve to hinder you. All you get living this way is constant stress and worry. You have to keep yourself on your toes and never let yourself slip up.

The reason you have to be on your toes is that you are making up a whole new persona. The way you are behaving is NOT the real you. You real personality will come to you effortlessly, which is precisely why it is so easy to make a mistake and slipup. Furthermore, when you don't say exactly what you feel, you end up with a lot of things bottled up inside you that need a valve for release. Trust me when I say this as I speak from experience. There are important feelings, emotions, thoughts, fights and compliments that just remain inside of you and keep you up long after you should have been asleep. What was it that was holding me back, preventing me from fully accepting who I was?

Why was the self-doubt so debilitating that I felt compelled to keep most of myself hidden? Maybe the fear of rejection and that of being ridiculed and shunned was so great that I could now no longer look at myself with compassion. I could not find it within myself to give myself a chance. After all those years, now that I wanted to be myself, I had ingrained in myself the idea that I was not worthy of being myself. Basically, I had come to resent myself.

This was the time I finally realized that enough was enough. I had to do something about this. I was, at this point, incapable of following my dreams and living life the way I wanted to because I did not trust myself in my version of what I felt life should have been like. Even thinking this was a difficult task. It was an extremely difficult task for me to find within myself the confidence to make a decision and stick with it. Of course, it is only natural to be concerned about your opinions and to double check to make sure that you are doing the right thing, the moral thing. However, it is not okay to handicap yourself into not taking any action at all. Furthermore, it is not acceptable to think that someone's opinion about you is the absolute truth.

"Always be yourself and have faith in yourself. Do not go out and look for a successful personality and try to duplicate it."

-Bruce Lee

This is one of the reasons that you should work on self-trust. If you trust yourself and find it within yourself to be completely honest and vulnerable with yourself, you give yourself freedom from the opinions of others. I used to struggle with it all the time. Instead of looking inwards, I used to look towards others' opinions about every aspect of my behavior to verify whether it was good or not. Let me tell you something, I have learned this the real hard way since I had no reference point for any of this. People, more often than not, are harsh judges.

If you judge yourself through their eyes, you will end up believing that you are a no good piece of junk that just gets in the way and does not trust anyone else. When you internalize these opinions, you tend to overlook all that is good in you, all that is unique and right about you. After a lot of internal struggle with my thoughts, I finally realized that I needed to be gentler with myself. I needed to let go of a few things and get back in touch with my inner self; the one I kept locked up for so long.

When I was trying to accomplish this, I realized that it was impossible to escape from your thoughts, which is not exactly a groundbreaking discovery. I am sure many before me have made a similar observation, however this made me realize that the only reason I was in this mess in the first place was because I couldn't find a way to escape from my thoughts and suppressing them only seemed to aggravate them further. Thus, I eventually ended up following them.

"The greatest gift you can give to somebody is your own personal development. I used to say, 'if you take care of me, I will take care of you.' Now I say, 'I will take care of me for you, if you take care of you for me.'"

-Jim Rohn

Becoming your own worst critic, taking on more than you can handle, saying *"Yes"* when you really want to say *"No"* are all signs that you are not trusting yourself. In addition to this, the biggest reason you have for not trusting yourself is that you have sabotaged your own life. You are the one who thought that you were not good enough, so you kept everything bottled up inside yourself.

You were the one who thought it would be a good idea to think to yourself repeatedly that you had to act in life in order to keep your real self-hidden, just because you feared that you might get rejected. Finally, you were the one who thought it would be a good idea to form rigid routines that leave no room for fun in your life. All you start doing as you grow up is start following blindly all that you have seen around yourself.

You, like all those around you, start working on the system of delayed gratification. You hold off on the dessert until you have finished a whole portion of veggies. Just like your parents did with you while growing up.

"To be yourself in a world that is constantly trying to make you something else is the greatest accomplishment."

-Ralph Waldo Emerson

What most of us, including myself, didn't realize at that time was that delayed gratification would make me my worst enemy. While all the incessant questioning and distrust of others was used as an excuse for not trusting myself to react well, delayed gratification became the reason that sealed the door of self-distrust. When I started beating myself up and dwelling on all the things that I did wrong, I was setting up the stage for the final act of self-distrust.

After all that I had done, I added to the damage by

allowing myself to dwell on my past mistakes, and I made sure that I was hard on myself. In fact, very soon, I started associating being miserable as the only way I was able to motivate myself. I started internalizing that if I beat myself up enough, I would be able to achieve success. So, after leading such a chaotic life of self-distrust, how was it that I emerged pretty fine on the other end? The truth is that nobody escapes from this at all, let alone be fine at the end of it. Not trusting yourself gives you the biggest sense of disappointment that you can ever feel. All because it is internalized. You are the one who is thinking and feeling everything. It is inside you yourself that you can feel such a wide range of emotions that are constantly at war with each other.

On the one hand, you want to feel happy, but you also don't want to come to a place where your productivity falls. At the same time, you so not want to take chances with the people around you in case someone hurts you. Secondly, you want to protect yourself from becoming a joke, so you isolate yourself. You have giving yourself so many reasons about you not being capable enough that the result is a devastating amount of weight that settles on your chest and threatens to spill over.

"Talk to yourself like you would to someone you love."

-Brené Brown

When I realized that I was self-sabotaging my own life with the way I thought, I tried to learn everything I can so that I wouldn't keep repeating my mistakes. I wanted to become free from all the unwanted burdens that I placed on myself and live a life that God intended. By setting myself up with rewards for being productive or accomplishing a certain task, in essence repeating the patterns of my childhood, I ensured that I would keep achieving the same results that my younger self kept delivering.

I think most of you out there would agree that your rebellious phase was directly connected to you not understanding why you needed to do certain things in a certain way. This lack of understanding is why you rebelled. Well, I did the same thing with my older self as well. However, now, it was much more harmful. I tried to make myself do something purely on the basis of rewards, without trying to understand the reason, and because of that I rebelled internally like a child.

The result had been the development of deep distrust of my own self. So, after a few painful years, I realized that I had to break free of this cycle if I ever hoped to achieve anything with my life. So after educating myself on the topic of self-trust, I finally gathered a few important things that are essential for anyone who wants to break free from similar patterns. The most important thing to realize is that you need to have people around you whom you can trust. You need to be able to confide your thoughts to them. You need to feel connected with them, and they should inspire within you a feeling of comfort and security. The more comfortable you feel with them, the more you will feel comfortable with yourself. This is the first step. You need to slowly but surely find a way to achieve this; a group of people to surround yourself with that you trust deeply.

The second thing that is helpful when trying to break free and start trusting yourself is talking. You need to put into words what you are feeling and thinking. That is why you need to surround yourself with people you trust. When you talk to them about your feelings, they not only need to listen, but they also respond to what you are saying.

This will help you find meaningful connections, and will be more than just validating your thoughts. You need these positive people to encourage your positive thinking by adding their own thoughts and ideas to yours. It is a neurologically proven point that talking to someone about your problems can change the neurological makeup of your brain and help you view the problem differently. It is true that after a lifetime of distrust, you will not find these steps easy. However, you need to learn how to recognize people who you can trust. The next step is you letting yourself work through everything. You need to accept that you will make mistakes, and that is something you have no control over. You, however, have complete control over what you do after you have made a mistake. Your response to the mistake is something you have to work on. Learn from it and move on. Dwelling on it will not change it.

You need to understand that practice is what is going to help you in the long run. No one is born knowing how to accomplish something. Everyone learns, although each and every individual has their own pace. In addition to this, you need to understand that in order for you to trust someone, you first have to become trustworthy. You have to give to others and behave with them the way you would like them to behave with you.

You should teach yourself how to recognize the needs of

others through nonverbal cues. You should try to help those around you without sacrificing your own needs. This is something I cannot emphasize enough. When you try to fulfill the needs of those around you, you should first set limits and boundaries that you will not cross in trying to fulfill their needs. Following these simple yet profound rules, I have changed my life for the better. These few things helped me to learn to trust myself and change my life for the better.

"Once we believe in ourselves, we can risk curiosity, wonder, spontaneous delight, or any experience that reveals the human spirit."

-E.E. Cummings

Chapter 6 - Taking The Risk And Going For What You Want

"He who is not courageous enough to take risks in life will accomplish nothing in life."

-Muhammad Ali

Most of us have goals in our minds that come with a lot of risks. Life may be all about taking risks, but not everyone is willing to take them. We miss a lot of great opportunities offered to us by life due to our fear of taking risks. There are people who risk their lives for the sake of others. And there are some people, like me, who can't even risk their careers in order to pursue their dreams. Taking a risk means feeling the fear, but doing it anyways. If we spend most of our time giving into our fears, we can barely call that living a life.

How many of us have cowered under the pressure of 'what ifs' that forced us to make the wrong decisions? How many of us spent restless nights wondering what life would be like had we seized that particular life-changing moment, instead of completely avoiding it? How long are we willing to spend the rest of our lives wondering? Be honest with yourself and ask yourself whether the life you are currently living really is truly worth living for.

I do not mean to trigger any negative thoughts in your mind through these questions, but I know how inevitable it really is to not feel sad when you accept your reality. How can we overcome our fear of taking risks? How do we let go of the fear that is holding us back from achieving our goals and dreams? Well, that answer solely depends on you and how willing you are to change your life.

Take the Risk or Lose the Chance

Taking risks often comes with guaranteed changes. The part that comes after accepting that change is taking the risk. Most of us lose a lot of chances in our life due to our fear of taking risks. We lose our dream jobs because we are too afraid to leave our current jobs. We end up with toxic friends because we are afraid of making new ones. We drop our self-worth until we think we have no value. It is not easy to accept that our reality is a product of the chance that we call fate. If we are not willing to take any chances, then are we truly living our lives to the fullest? Maybe taking risks involves endangering an environment that you are familiar with.

It is in human nature to accept the environment once we are adjusted to it. We miss out on once-in-a-lifetime-opportunities simply because we do not have enough confidence in ourselves. We doubt ourselves for everything and berate ourselves. It is time to stop questioning yourself over little things and just take a leap with high hopes.

"If you are not willing to risk the unusual, you will have to settle for the ordinary."

-Jim Rohn

Being ordinary is not the problem here. Being unsatisfied with being ordinary is the actual problem. There is nothing wrong with being ordinary as long as you are happy with it.

I am not saying that ordinary is bad, either. No, most people in this life want to be nothing but ordinary. But if being ordinary is something that annoys you, makes you question your self-worth, upsets you every time you think about it, then maybe it is time to reevaluate your life again. Mainly because dissatisfaction in life leads us towards the wrong path. The more we search for something to make up for that dissatisfaction, the more we find ourselves falling down a black hole. Sometimes, you need to take huge risks to make your life extraordinary.

Let Go of 'What If' and Focus on 'What Is'

I have missed out a lot of great chances to make myself happy solely based on the 'what ifs' mantra in my head. Before taking a chance, I find myself asking the same question over and over again.

"What if it doesn't work out this time? What if something goes wrong? What if I fail to meet the expectations of others? What if I'm not good enough to finish this task? What if... what if... what if?"

If you are someone who understands the 'what ifs'

mantra, then you must be just like me. You tire yourself out worrying about things that have not even happened yet. You worry about the future, things that are completely uncertain. You end up focusing more on 'what ifs' instead of enjoying 'what is'. What I mean is, you don't enjoy your present as much as you worry about your future. You lose sight of your goals somewhere along the way, until you completely forget about them. Your goals end up remaining as 'dreams' instead of your 'reality' for the rest of your life. Are you really going to let that happen to you? Why are you harming yourself by worrying about something that is not even guaranteed to even happen?

As someone wise once said, you only live once (YOLO). None of us will get another chance to live our life again. Do we really want to live this life merely worrying about something we don't even know is going to happen? It is better to say, "*I can't believe I did that,*" instead of saying, "*I wish I did that.*"

Maybe it is time to finally get out of our one-tracked minds and explore other opportunities. What is the worst that can happen? If we make a choice with complete resolution, then why do we regret it? In the end, we mostly only end up regretting the chances we didn't take.

How Can We be Sure That We Made the Right Choice if We Do Not Take a Risk?

We mostly end up fantasizing about how our life would be if we had made that one particular decision that involved risking something. Whether it was a refusal to a job proposal or an agreement to marry the person you love, we all question the decisions we made somewhere along the end of the road. You end up asking yourselves what the person living in your alternative universe would be like if you hadn't made that one small decision.

But how can we really be sure that we made the right decision if we don't take risks? How can we be sure that we made the right choice by actually taking the risk? Perhaps you want to take a risk, but are too afraid of what the people will say; what the society will say; what everyone around you is going to say.

You worry about this so much that it stops you from doing what you want. But have you ever wondered what your future-self would say when they think back on this moment? **Why are we so afraid of disappointing others,**

but not afraid of disappointing ourselves? Most of us avoid great opportunities due to the fear of disappointing others. But what about you? Why do you want to spend the rest of your life regretting and disappointing yourself? Don't be afraid to take the risks and see where that lands you. Even if that leads you into a bad situation, you can satisfy yourself by saying that you at least gave it a try. When a person does not try at all, they end up regretting and wondering about it for the rest of their lives. It is better to get over with something rather than spending the rest of your life wondering about it.

"It always seems impossible until it is done."

-Nelson Mandela

There are going to be a lot of people in your life who are going to laugh in your face when you actually tell them what you are planning to do in your life. In fact, sometimes, those who are closest to our hearts ridicule us. Being ridiculed by your loved ones is more than enough to make you give up on that idea altogether.

You tell yourself that you will never go on with that plan.

Or you can grow the courage to take their ridicule as a challenge and show them that you do have the courage to believe in yourself. Our dreams always seem impossible until we actually take the initiative for achieving them. Do not tell yourself how impossible something is going to be. How you will never make it to the end. How everything is going to be all for nothing in the end. No, stop telling yourself that you cannot do it.

That your idea is completely bullocks. Even the word 'impossible' says 'I'm Possible'. It all depends on how we look at the world around us. Our mindset also plays an important role in helping us. The more positive outlook we have on life, the more likely we are to achieve our dreams.

Failure Is a Part of Success

Failure comes with a lot of life lessons. Experiencing failure once in your life teaches you a lesson that you end up remembering for the rest of your life. I used to get disheartened by the failures I have experienced in my life. But then, I remembered how failing has made me wise enough to guide someone else.

Through this book, I will be able to guide you regarding

the pros and cons involving risks. The first thing one must keep in mind is that life is like a never ending game. If you win, you will be happy. But if you lose, you will be *wise*. There are no cons in life regarding failure if one is willing to learn from it. We hold ourselves back in fear of failing without realizing that failure prepares us for the bigger picture. It may be better to be safe than sorry, but it is never better to fear failure and miss out an opportunity. Sometimes, we need to get out of our safety blankets to live out the raw experiences of this world. It can be scary at first because you have mostly lived out your life cocooned in that safety blanket.

The first step is to break free from your safety blanket as it holds you back from a lot of life-changing opportunities. Most people make the mistake of convincing themselves that everything is going to be okay. Stop hoping for nothing but the best. Sometimes, you will not end up receiving the results that you were anticipating. Instead, prepare yourself for the worst to come before stepping out of your comfort zone. Your comfort zone may keep you safe, but you will never be able to grow in that zone.

You will never be able to make progress if you do not step out and actually do what you want. To see yourself grow, get yourself out there in the field. Knowing that things can go wrong, and they *do* go wrong, sometimes prepares us for the worst outcomes. At least we are not sad or disappointed by the negative outcome. You can simply move on and forget about it in the future because you know that you made an effort on your part. Preparation is vital before taking a leap of faith. Do not expect too much out of the chance you are willing to take, and instead tell yourself that you will make out, one way or another. Failure is truly a success if you are willing to learn from it. Whether you learn it the easy way or the hard way, you should understand how to accept it one way or another in order to move on.

The Biggest Risks Are the Ones You Do Not Take

There are two types of risks in this world. The risks that you take for your own sake, and the risks that you don't take. I am not saying that you should actually jump in the middle of traffic and call it taking a 'risk'. Many of you might feel like it is no less than that when it comes to making a decision. But it is better than being stuck on a pathway.

Carve your own way in this life instead of following others. Discover yourself and form your own identity. As stated in the first chapter of the book, ask yourself who you really are. Let us take a look at the worlds famous millionaires. Their rags to riches stories have always inspired me to take risks in life. They always believed in their dreams and actually made it by investing in it. These stories tell us that there is nothing wrong with dreaming about things that only we can see.

"In a world that is changing really quickly, the only strategy that is guaranteed to fail is not taking risks."

-Mark Zuckerberg

Mark Zuckerberg has often shared his experience of failing with the now famous website known as 'Facebook' over and over again until he got it right. He went out of his way to create a platform that connected people all over the world for free. Mark Zuckerberg took a risk to achieve his dreams by believing in himself.

"All our dreams can come true if we have the courage to

pursue them."

-Walt Disney

We all grew up watching Walt Disney's animation films as children. Most of our childhood dreams were inspired by those cartoons. But not most of us know how many times Walt Disney rose and fell during the first years. From facing bankruptcy to earning millions of dollars, Walt Disney never stopped believing in himself and his dreams.

"Success is a lousy teacher. It seduces smart people into thinking they can't lose."

-Bill Gates

Let us talk about Bill Gates. He completely transformed the world of computers by introducing Microsoft Software. He managed to shock the whole world. The only reason why we have the updated version of this software is because he never stopped looking for ways to improve it.

Success had been achieved while self-satisfaction was nowhere to be found.

We all recognize him as one of the top ten richest billionaires in this world. You might know that this man dropped out of high school when he was merely a teenager. Yet, he turned out to be far more successful than those who actually graduated from his school. While he owns Microsoft Software, one of his smart classmates works for him as the manager. So, how did Bill Gates manage to actually create something that no one could even ever think of creating? It's simple. He merely went out of his way and risked his pubescent years into creating a better future; not just for himself, but for the future of computers. He firmly believes that success only coaxes smart and intelligent people into thinking that they are always going to come out winning.

Whereas, in reality, not everyone is fortunate enough to succeed during their first trial. Through countless failures, we can learn how to correct our errors in many ways and to not make the same mistake twice. Those who easily win are also those who are easily disheartened when they lose. Don't be easily disappointed by setbacks.

Instead, come up with countless ideas to overcome those setbacks. When we start treating our life's setback as challenges, it is when we truly start to enjoy life. It makes one wonder, how many of us have prevented ourselves from reaching our full potential without even realizing it? How many of us have berated ourselves until we are convinced that we cannot amount to anything? The answer may be too shocking to face.

Stop Holding Yourself Back

The biggest mistake most of us make in life is that we hold ourselves back from reaching our full potential. Most of us hold ourselves back from making that one decision, one choice, one statement that could have completely transformed our lives. I have friends who have confided in me and told me how they regret the things they never do. It's always about the opportunities they missed and the risks they didn't take.

Regret, more often than not, actually stems from what we did not do rather than what we did. Why is that? Why do we always end up regretting the chances we didn't take? Is it because we are left wondering what could have been instead? The worst part of not taking risks is allowing them to prevent you from getting your happiness. You let your fears deprive you from contentment.

That is one of the reasons why we are always stuck wondering about the things we don't do, things we don't say, and the risks we don't take. We hold ourselves back from achieving true happiness. It is mainly because we are not content with the life we are leading. You know that life is too short to spend it regretting. A life spent regretting is not a life well spent living.

You are merely living for the sake of living. Why not try living for the sake of trying? We need to live *in* order to find a reason to live *for*. How are we going to find that reason if we are not willing to take risks? Do not hold yourself back from doing what you want. Seize the moments you have been waiting for all your life.

Only you can help yourself in overcoming your fears of taking risks. Get out there in the real world and take what's yours with your head held high. Do not think about what will come after it. Live in the moment and forget about the past. Stop shutting yourself in a box. You will only end up suffocating yourself while worrying about your future.

I always think about how the adults in my life repeatedly told me to think outside the box, while conveniently forgetting that we were taught to color inside the lines. It is time to break free of such lines that are holding you back from making your life colorful.

It is essential to acknowledge the fact that life is made up of endless opportunities. Do not let these opportunities pass by. Take control of your own life and step up your game. Believe in yourself, and invest in your future, by taking risks in the moment.

It is better to be labelled as adventurous rather than being labelled as predictable. Nothing is worse than living and repeating the same old pattern. It is only natural for you to get tired of living in a loop of regrets and missed opportunities. Put your efforts and heart into this life, and watch the achievements fall into your steps.

Think strategically, but not statistically. Do not be afraid of becoming one of the statistics. Go out and travel the whole world. Choose the career you have always been dreaming of. Be the person you wanted by your side. Support your own dreams and aspirations. Chase your dreams, even after you become breathless.

It is never too late to turn your life around. Overcome your fear of taking risks and witness the progress you make in your life. We are granted with this one life, one opportunity, to turn it completely around. Start experiencing your life because in the end, we only regret the chances we did not take and the risks we were not ready to make.

"If it is still in your mind, it is worth taking the risk."

-*Paulo Coelho*

Chapter 7 - Loving Yourself Unconditionally

"Love yourself. Forgive yourself. Be true to yourself. How you treat yourself sets the standard for how others will treat you."

-Steve Maraboli, Unapologetically You: Reflections on Life and the Human Experience

It is a common thing these days to find people who are just too insecure about themselves. Far too often, people forget that they are the ones who have to look after themselves. No one else is going to come and do it for them. You are the one who has to pick up the slack when your mind, body, and soul are feeling down. How else do you expect yourself to lead a life that is content? That is the whole point of my book; to make you realize that **YOU** are important. I want you to know that you are the only one who can take your care to the next level.

The thing is that self-care, self-worth, self-esteem, self-awareness, and self-confidence are just different aspect of one thing: your ability to live life well and to the fullest. If you have a healthy level of all the things I have mentioned above, only then you have provided yourself with the tools to live a well-respected, happy and prosperous life. Loving yourself means a variety of things and comes with many different aspects to it.

Loving yourself includes the way you treat yourself and others, setting boundaries and limits, self-awareness, and demanding respect. I want you to also be aware that you are not able to love anyone if you don't know how to love yourself properly first. Think about it. How is it possible for you to give something that you don't have? For example, if you have $0 and someone asks you for $10, how are you supposed to be able to give it to them?

Similarly, you cannot make anyone love you the way you want to be loved. You have to first love yourself, which is when you set the standard for someone else to love you. If you are low on your own list of priorities then how can you expect someone else to place you higher? I know that this logic might seem counter-intuitive, but trust me, that is the way it is.

Even when you are taking care of someone else above your own self, and loving them more than you love yourself, it in no way makes them prioritize you. This is despite what logic and common courtesy would dictate that if you have made them a priority, they should afford you the same courtesy. Nonetheless, that is not the case. You have to show everyone around you that this is how you are willing to treat yourself and others.

That you would be willing to go an extra mile for them, but that is just it. It is going to be only a mile, nothing more than that. You have to set a limit, draw your boundaries, and stick to them. If you forgo the limit even once, you are once again setting yourself up to be taken advantage of.

"I have never listened to anyone who criticized my taste in space travel, sideshows or gorillas. When this occurs, I pack up my dinosaurs and leave the room."

-Ray Bradbury, Zen in the Art of Writing

That is what happens when you keep taking care of others. They just start expecting it from you. They do not even think twice before they have fallen into the habit of using you. However, it is not their fault, as this is human nature. Rather, the fault lies with you for making them comfortable enough so that they do not think before using you. If you are adamant about your limits and boundaries, then they would know that you have certain standards and rules that you are not willing to break.

That if they test you beyond a certain limit, they are just going to push you away. You have to tell them, through your actions, that the most important thing to you is your own sense of self-worth and that you know where to draw the line when it comes to handing out favors or even looking after your loved ones. How much are you going to do for one person? People need to be taught that they have a responsibility towards themselves.

No one can just fully depend on you to take care of their daily lives. You have the right to say no and those who want to stay in your life need to respect you turning them down every once in a while. Like I said, I was also ensnared in the trap of looking after other people, and my own welfare came after everyone else's. For me, there was no question as to who I should choose first as the answer was never me. That is, until the day I spent so much of myself for others that I started to feel empty inside. It was one of the scariest moments of my life. I kept feeling that way month after month, and those were the hardest days of my life. I did not know why I was feeling this empty and how I could go back to being like my usual self. During those months, I reminisced about my cheerful attitude. I tried to recalled how happy I used to be, and did my best to remember some of it again, but all to no avail.

"Be who you are and say what you feel, because those who mind don't matter, and those who matter don't mind."

-Bernard M. Baruch

It is really hard to put what I was feeling into words, and I was trying very hard to verbalize my feelings. The reason was that I wanted to hear out loud what I was feeling, as I was very unsettled by it. For a few weeks, I struggled with it and had a hard time. So I tried to use analogies to explain my feelings. It was this analogy, that I am about to share with you as well, that helped me get out of the hole I had dug for myself. I was feeling like I was a jug of water and for some time in my life, I had water poured into me. Then, I had poured water out into other jugs as well: the jug being me and water being feelings. However, for the recent part of my life, I had been the one pouring water out while not having enough poured into me. So now, I was just this empty jug. As soon I put that into words, I realized what a game I had been playing with my life.

I just poured out everything I had, while people had given me very little in return. In fact, the more I poured out my emotions into them, the less they responded back to me. It was this time of my life that I realized I had just set myself up for this emptiness. However, I was not going to take this lying down either. I was going to learn from this huge mistake and make sure that those who come after me, or are currently following in the footsteps of my previous self, do not commit the same mistakes.

I want you to be able to fall in love with yourself, and never break the connection that your body has with your soul and your mind. You loving yourself is the one thing that will pave the way for the best life that you can lead. For everything is connected to this one little thing, self-love. Its presence will make your life not only better, but meaningful. Its absence, on the other hand, will not only make your life pointless, but also unnecessarily hard and painful.

"When you are able to love yourself deeply, you can be kind to others."

-Debasish Mridha

This speaks to my soul because I know how hard it is to be kind or happy if you do not love yourself enough. If you feel like you do not deserve the right to be happy. That you have nothing to offer to those around you. It can be a hard thing to love those who are around you. My point in telling you this is that I see so many people who do not appreciate themselves enough. Subconsciously, they're thinking that they do not matter as much as someone else does.

Even though self-love is a much-discussed topic these days, people just don't get the importance of it. Most people don't even realize that they are not loving themselves properly! Loving yourself is more than just knowing that you're beautiful or attractive. It is an attitude; the way you carry yourself; the boundaries you set for yourself and others. It is knowing that without taking care of yourself and your wellbeing FIRST, you are not able to do anything for anyone else. It is not putting yourself in situations that will not benefit you in the future. It is making the right choices that are healthy and conducive to your life. It is having the confidence to trust and believe in yourself, and going for what you want. It is not letting other's negative words tear you down and letting other's insecurities take away from your shine.

Just imagine the magnitude of our folly: how we are wasting our lives just because we do not have the courage to love ourselves. Just because we are not strong enough to be introspective and self-aware enough to make a difference in our own lives. While most of us want to make a difference in this world, we don't realize that that effort starts with ourselves. Self-awareness is described as having a clear perception of yourself.

Now *"your-self"* is something that includes your personality, your individuality, your strengths as well as your weaknesses, your thoughts, your beliefs, your motivations, and your emotions. Self-awareness is realizing where you stand with each and every one of your traits. As I discovered, and am still discovering, on my journey towards self-improvement, the layers of self-awareness are just endless. You might think you understand yourself, but the more you look inwards, the more complex *"yourself"* becomes. I thought that I was sufficiently self-aware, and did not need to delve any deeper. I mean I know I was no yogi or anything like that, but I did think that I knew myself to actually make informed decisions about life that would be good for me. Turns out that this the trap we all fall into. I see so many people who could have avoided this trap if they just realized they needed to connect with themselves a little more deeply.

As you become more self-aware, you are able to identify your thought patterns. In doing so, you gain the ability to make changes in them, which in turn allows you to control your emotions. For my part, I think that is where we encounter most of our problems; in our emotional responses as either we get too emotional, or we don't feel enough. Most of the time, we are not able to balance our emotional response and maintain it according to the situation. That, in turn, escalates the situation, which otherwise would have been a mild or even a pleasant one.

"In order to be irreplaceable, one must always be different."

-Coco Chanel

When you strive to become self-aware, you are taking the first step in mastering your life. Wherever you focus your attention, emotions and thoughts are where you are most likely to end up. If, for example, you are thinking negative thoughts, you are most likely to end up in negative situations. Another example I want you to share with you is that even if you think you are making the right decision, and you do not have positive thoughts and emotions to back it up, then even the most perfect of situations can fall apart on you.

Your thoughts decide the type of life you are going to lead. Hence, even the choice of your life partner depends upon your thoughts and emotions. If you are feeling positive, you attract positive people to yourself, and vice versa. If you are going through an emotional turmoil, being self-aware can be a difficult thing, as your body loses touch with your mind and soul. The best analogy that I have ever read on how to become self-aware is that trying to become self-aware is like learning to dance.

While you are learning to dance, there is a whole slew of things that you have to pay attention to; where your feet are moving, how you have to move your body, how you have to sync up with your partner, as well as the beats of the music. That is kind of like how you try to be self-aware as well. You cannot learn to dance from a book. You have to see and feel the movements with all your senses.

Self-awareness is what you develop when you are aware of your expressions and your thoughts in accordance with your emotions and behavior. Now that I have explained the most important aspect of self-love, which is self-awareness, let's get back to understanding what self-love truly is. Self-love is not something that can be achieved if you pamper yourself for a while and go get yourself a new set of clothes or a makeover.

It is not something you get by reading something motivational or inspirational, nor is it something that you can get by being in a new and wonderful relationship. For self-love is not just a state of feeling good. Self-love is a state of being that stems from being appreciative of actions that support our physical, psychological and spiritual growth. Self-love is dynamic.

It is something that, as it increases in us, makes us more accepting of our strengths, as well as weaknesses. Like I said before, **there are too many people out there who do not understand the value and potential they hold. That is what self-love fixes**. It shows you what strengths you possess, while at the same time it makes you accept your weaknesses without getting defensive about them.

Through my own struggle with self-love and self-awareness, I have found a few things that have helped me in opening myself up and becoming more self-aware and having more self-love. The first step in achieving that is to become mindful. People who have more self-love tend to know what they think, feel and want. They are always aware of who they are and they keep fast on this knowledge and do not stray into the trap of what others want from them.

The next step towards you becoming more self-aware and loving yourself is when you realize that you need to act on WHAT YOU NEED rather than focusing on what you want. When you turn away from something that feels good and exciting towards something that you need in your life to stay strong and move forward, that is when you love yourself. By becoming more aware of what you want and what you need, you are taking a giant step towards getting out of patterns that get you into trouble. Consequently, you stop doubting yourself and it lessens self-distrust. It is very important that you break free of this cycle. In addition when acting on what you need rather than what you want, you also want to take good care of yourself. The premise here is that if your basic needs are met properly by you, then you stand a much better chance of loving yourself. It is rather easy to understand if you think of yourself as two people.

One that is needy, and the other who is in charge. The one in charge is you. Even though the needy one is you as well, in this example, that version of you is now the second party, who has control over your thoughts and emotions. In order to keep your thoughts and emotions well balanced, you need to take care of the needy self.

Even though this example might be a bit uncomfortable, once you get used to the idea that you have to take care of the needy side of you, you will be that much closer to achieving a higher standard of self-love. Furthermore, you need to set boundaries. This one applies to everyone, including yourself. You will definitely love yourself more when you set limits and learn to say *"No."*

You need to learn to say no to any situation that you want to, be it love, work or anything that you feel is draining your energy more than it is giving you any other benefits that you are seeking. Any activity that makes you go out of sync with your emotional and spiritual self must be avoided, as well as anything that you think is a poor representation of yourself. For example, if you think the exercise routine that you are doing is draining you more than it is benefiting you, then it is something that you should stop.

Try to change up the routine or your surroundings to see if that helps. Do not, by any means, give up exercise. Rather, try to find something that represents who you are, and who you want to become. Then figure out what type of routine you should be following. Additionally, the most important aspect is to protect yourself by bringing the right people into your life.

That is something I cannot stress enough. People who surround you are a reflection of what your mind and soul are becoming as it is getting influenced by them, so good people will reflect positivity onto your mind and soul while others will drain your mental, physical as well as spiritual energy, leaving you feeling exhausted and unable to focus on your needs. There is a good analogy for this as well. Imagine that you had a friend who sold perfume, and another friend who sold coal. Now without thinking about their characters or personalities as a judging criteria, and only judging on their occupations, think about who you would want to spend the majority of your time with. The perfume seller, right. Spending time with him or her, you will enjoy yourself by sitting in a pleasant and aromatic atmosphere and when you leave them, you will be surrounded by the aroma of different perfumes.

You will be giving off a fragrant smell as well. On the other hand, if you are sitting with the coal seller, you will not only be miserable while sitting with him, as there would be coal dust everywhere. The atmosphere would not be conducive towards making you happy as there won't be anything cheerful to look at. There will only be black coals, and when you leave, your clothes will be black from the coal dust and you will be smelling like the acrid smell that is unique to coals.

That is kind of like how you want to protect your mind and soul from people who are selling coal. Another aspect of protecting yourself is described best with a term that is coined by newer generations, *'frenemies'*. This describes the friends who take pleasure in your pain, and these are the second type of people who you want to avoid. You do not have the time to waste on people who want to disrupt anything good that you have going on in your life. The next thing that you want to be doing is being gentle and forgiving towards yourself. As humans, either we are looking to avoid confrontation with our shortcoming or we are on our own case 24/7. Due to this, we end up judging ourselves too harshly. That is why most people avoid confrontation with their own weaknesses and avoid taking responsibility.

The result of that in most cases is that we find it very hard to forgive ourselves. We do not think to learn and grow from our mistakes, and instead we get lost in the regret of ever having committed it in the first place. The thing is that at some point, you have to accept that you are only human. By that, I mean you are going to make mistakes and that is how you are going to grow: by learning from them.

When you start on your journey towards more self-love,

you need to practice being less hard on yourself and remember that the mistake is not the end of your life. As long as you are breathing, you have another chance. There are no failures, only lessons learned. Lastly, you need to live with a resolute INTENTION. You will open up more space to love yourself and accept yourself more if you live purposefully, and have an overall idea of your thoughts and the path that you are moving towards. Although by that, I do not mean that you need to have a firm plan and everything figured out about your life. What you need is to have figured out how you are going to react and the general direction that you want your life to move in. The simple thing is you will love yourself more if you see yourself accomplishing the goals that you set out with. If you give yourself a purpose and feel productive, you will invite in more self-love.

These are just a few points that will get you started on your journey of self-love. You have to then figure out what works best for you and stick with it. Just imagine how much your life will change if you start practicing just a couple of these pointers. Take baby steps, you will get there. I know that because I have done it, too!

Quotes of Inspiration

"Do what you have to do until you can do what you want to do."

-Oprah Winfrey

"You can get to where you want to be from wherever you are but you must stop spending so much time noticing and talking about what you do not like about where you are."

-A. Hicks

"Be yourself... No one can ever tell you you're doing it wrong"

-James L. Herlihy

"The only thing standing between you and your goal is the bullshit story you keep telling yourself as to why you can't achieve it."

-Jordan Belfort

"When you want to succeed as bad as you want to breathe, then you'll be successful."

-Eric Thomas

"You can't go back and chance the beginning, but you can start where you are and change the ending."

-C.S. Lewis

"Change the way you look at things and things you look at will begin to change."

-Wayne Dyer

"Our Anxiety does not come from thinking about the future, but from wanting to control it."

-Kahil Gibran

"Every situation in life is temporary. So, when life is good, make sure you enjoy and receive it fully. And when life is not so good, remember that it will not last forever and better days are on the way."

-Jenni Young

"People take different roads seeking fulfillment and happiness. Just because they're not on your road doesn't mean they've gotten lost."

-Dalai Lama XIV

"Be True to yourself and be Genuine to others Attract what you expect, Reflect what you desire, become who you respect, mirror what you admire"

-Unknown

"I used to walk into a room full of people and wonder if they liked me... Now I took around and wonder if I like them."

-Unknown

"If you're always trying to be normal, you will never know

how amazing you can be."

-Unknown

"Life isn't about waiting for the storm to pass, it's about learning to dace in the rain"

-Vivian Greene

"Don't compare your life with others. There is no comparison between the sun and the moon They shine when it's their time."

-Cassey Ho

"I'm still determined to be happy, regardless of what life throws at me. I have learned through experience that my happiness will depend on my attitude and mind set, not my circumstances. I choose to be happy!"

-Dave Hedges

"Happiness is an attitude of mind, born of the simple determination to be happy under all outward circumstances."

-J. Donald Walters

"A failure is not always a mistake, it may simply be the best one can do under the circumstances. The real mistake is to stop trying."

-B. F. Skinner

"If you get your ego in your way, you will only look to other people and circumstances to blame."

-Jocko Willink

"Feeling sorry for ourselves is the most useless waste of energy on the planet. It does absolutely no good. We can't let our circumstances or what others do or don't do control us. We can decide to be happy regardless."

-Joyce Meyer

JACK IN THE BOX

JACK IN THE BOX